Contents

All programmes are subtitled on Teletext for the deaf and hearing-impaired.

	A Victorian Diary and the curriculum		2
	Curriculum grid		3
Programme 1	**School Days**		4
	Factfile	Victorian schools	6
	Activity sheet 1	A school log book	7
	Activity sheet 2	Copperplate writing	8
Programme 2	**Downstairs, Upstairs**		9
	Factfile	Domestic service	11
	Activity sheet 3	A census return	12
	Activity sheet 4	Advertisements	13
Programme 3	**Down but not Out**		14
	Factfile	Victorian living and working conditions	16
	Activity sheet 5	Letter writing	17
	Activity sheet 6	Victorian houses	18
Programme 4	**Strike**		19
	Factfile	Factory working conditions	21
	Activity sheet 7	A Victorian biography	22
	Activity sheet 8	The Picture Magazine	23
Programme 5	**Final Chapter**		24
	Factfile	Victorian entertainment and leisure	26
	Activity sheet 9	Inventions of the century	27
	Additional resources		28
	Credits		Inside back cover
	Transmission and resources		Insert

We are always pleased to receive constructive comments and suggestions about both the series and the support materials. Please write to me at the address below.
Adrienne Jones Education Officer Channel 4 Learning PO Box 100 Warwick CV34 6TZ

A VICTORIAN DIARY
INTRODUCTION

Using the unit

Structure and content

The 5 x 15-minute programmes present the popular historical topic of the Victorians in the form of a diary written by the principal character, Maggie Johnson.

When we first meet Maggie Johnson it is 31 December 1899. Writing her diary on the eve of a new century, she begins to reminisce about her life and leads us back on a retrospective journey over the previous couple of decades.

It was at school in the north of England when, aged ten years, Maggie was first encouraged by her teacher to write a diary. From 15 October 1877, she kept an account of her life. The diary proved to be a wonderful outlet for the shy, young Maggie to describe personal events that happened to her and how she felt about them and later to document some of the social changes that took place.

The curriculum

The main focus of the unit is history, providing teachers with an opportunity to concentrate on historical knowledge and skills. This includes a glimpse of what it was like being at school at the end of the nineteenth century and gives an insight into children's lives then.

A glance at the curriculum grid on the opposite page enables teachers to identify the broad historical focus of each programme as well as other related subjects. By using the device of a diary to tell the story of everyday Victorian life, the programmes also offer an obvious literacy focus.

The Teachers' Guide

The Guide suggests ideas for discussion before each programme is viewed. This helps to establish children's current knowledge and encourages them to 'tune in' to what they are about to see. There is a 'factfile' in each section that provides additional information about the Victorian period and which can be photocopied.

The Guide identifies areas for the children to focus on while viewing, and gives suggestions for activities after viewing the programmes.

To complement the Teachers' Guide there is an Activity Book. It is a facsimile of Maggie's diary and is illustrated with photographs and pictures. It also includes ten photocopiable pupil sheets which are all based on literacy activities, particularly writing. With Maggie's diary having been written over a period of twenty-two years, it serves as a real example of extended writing!

curriculumgrid

Programme	Content	Outcomes
1. School Days	- distinctive features of a Victorian elementary school in the 1870s - similarities and differences between Victorian school life and that in schools today - genre of diary writing	**History:** copperplate writing, research **English:** writing, handwriting, keeping a diary, speaking and listening, note-taking **PSHE:** bullying discussion **D & T:** designing and making a cross-stitch sampler
2. Downstairs, Upstairs	- servants' way of life in Victorian times - differences between the lives of servants and those of their masters - typical features of Victorian houses and styles of decoration	**History:** domestic service, census return information, advertisements **English:** invitations **Art and design:** using a sketchbook, printing patterns, making a model Victorian room
3. Down but not Out	- impact of the railways - growth of cities - working and living conditions in Victorian London	**English:** drama (role-play), character, using writing frames – letter writing **History:** ICT population graph **D & T:** designing and making a model town
4. Strike	- important developments in Victorian employment and social history - changes in the lives and roles of working women - the impact of photography	**History:** lifestyle – studio portraits, famous Victorians **English:** play script, writing frames – biography, information texts, speaking and listening, speech bubbles **Art and design:** photography
5. Final Chapter	- importance of the Victorian era in advancing new technology and invention - chronological sequence of events during the Victorian age - Victorian forms of entertainment - story structure	**English:** research, note-taking, questions, non-narrative text, word-processing, poster design, writing a summary, imaginative writing **History:** comparing past and present **D & T:** designing and making a board game

A VICTORIAN DIARY
PROGRAMME 1

School Days

Programme outline

We are introduced to Maggie Johnson, writing her diary on the eve of the twentieth century. She tells us how she has kept her journals during Queen Victoria's reign, beginning when she was just ten years old. They trace the ups and downs of Maggie's life, and chronicle some of the social and technological developments of the Victorian era.

The programme then takes us back to the time of Maggie's schooldays at Stanton Elementary School – a board school in the north of England during the 1870s. We see the lessons taking place, witness Maggie's difficulties when she is bullied by an older girl and learn of the rigours, both for pupils and teachers, of the annual school inspection!

Learning outcomes

Children should gain an understanding of:

- the distinctive features of a Victorian elementary school in the 1870s
- vocabulary associated with education in Victorian times
- similarities and differences between Victorian school life and that in schools today
- the genre of diary writing
- the use of primary sources in gathering evidence about a historical period

Before viewing

- ☐ Discuss with the children what they already know about the Victorian era and Victorian schools in particular. What would they like to find out? Key questions for discussion could include:

    - What are the dates of the Victorian period?
    - Did all Victorian children go to school?
    - What subjects did they study?
    - Did boys and girls have the same lessons?
    - What happened if they misbehaved?

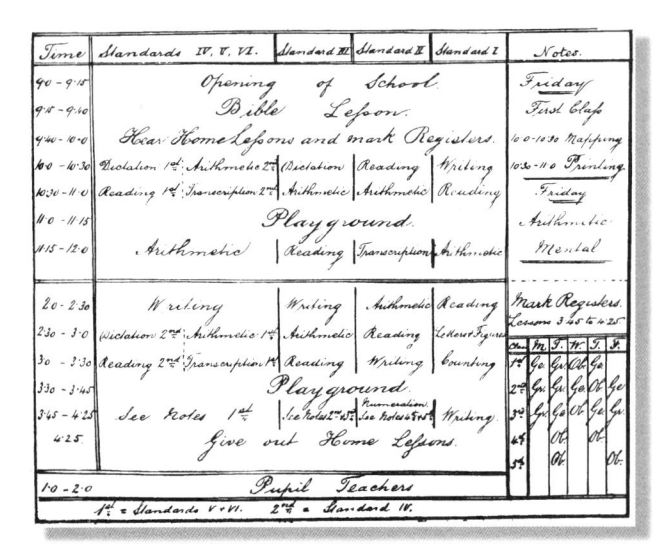

Whilst viewing

- ☐ Ask the children to make a list of any similarities or differences they spot between the school in the programme and their own primary school today.

After viewing

History

- ☐ Discuss with the children the notes they have made during the programme. On balance, would they choose to have been at school in Victorian times or to be at school today? Ask them to give reasons for their choices.

- During this period every school had to keep a daily log book of attendance and events. Ask the children to look at the extracts from a school log book in the 1890s on **Activity sheet 1** (page 7). Ideas for discussion could include:

    - Would the reasons given for non-attendance be acceptable today?
    - Would the headteacher have been pleased with the inspector's report?

- Many museums around the country organize workshops where children can dress up in Victorian costume and experience a Victorian school day. Should such a visit not be possible, why not arrange a Victorian day of your own in school. Photographs can help children research the kind of clothing that would have been worn by teacher and pupils. Choose a day when all of you dress up accordingly. On the day, the children might sit in rows, do sums in pounds, shillings and pence and practise their 'copperplate' handwriting using **Activity sheet 2** (page 8). After lunch the girls could design, and perhaps begin to make, a stitched 'sampler', while the boys might practise 'drill' in the playground. Ask the children how they feel about being split up like this.

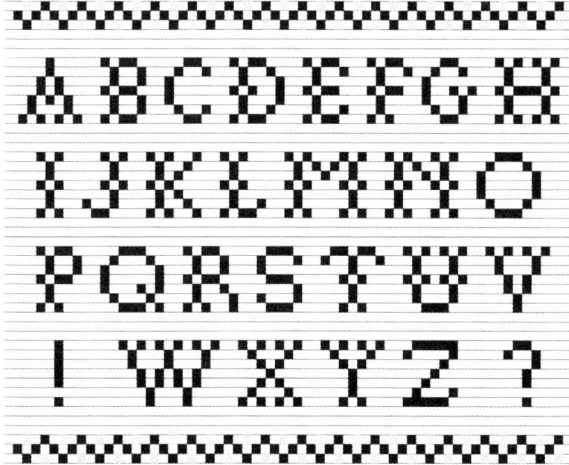

English: writing

- Read with the children the non-fiction passage about Victorian schools in the **factfile** (page 6). Ask the children to highlight two facts from each paragraph which could be included in their books or folders under the heading 'Did you know this about Victorian schools?' Was it fair that pupils had to remain in the same class after a poor inspection result, or that teachers could have part of their wages deducted?

    Then ask the children to pick out the following terms from the text so that they can each compile a glossary of their meanings:
    Education Act, board schools, monitor system, slates, copperplate handwriting.

- Discuss with the class the subject of keeping a diary. Do any of the children keep diaries or journals at present? Encourage them to each keep a personal diary for the next five weeks. Suggest that they include in their entries things that are personal to themselves, as well as current events, even world events, that they think might be of interest to people reading the diary in a hundred years' time. The children may want to include pictures and photographs, and it might be possible to set aside a regular time-slot each week for them to look through newspapers and magazines for relevant material.

- Mount a wall display using extracts from a selection of fictional and non-fictional diaries and journals. These might include the diaries of Anne Frank, Samuel Pepys, *The Country Diary of an Edwardian Lady* and *The Wreck of the Zanzibar* by Michael Morpurgo.

PSHE

- Maggie's experiences at school can be used to explore, either with the whole class, or with smaller groups, the sensitive issue of bullying. Maggie doesn't tell anyone about the problems she is having. Do the children think this is a wise course of action? How else could Maggie have dealt with the conflict? Examine these issues further through role-play, with class members 'improvising' different solutions. For example, what might happen as Maggie tells her mother and Miss Bates about her problems with Susan? A contemporary book useful in exploring these issues is *The Angel of Nitshill Road* by Anne Fine.

D & T

- Using the designs on the **factfile** for letters and borders, the children can design and make a cross-stitch sampler using squared paper and binka.

factfile

ictorian schools

At the start of Queen Victoria's reign many children did not go to school. Instead, they went out to work, mostly unable to read or write.
In 1870 an Act of Parliament, the Education Act, was passed, which said that all children between the ages of five and thirteen years could attend school if they paid the sum of 1d (one penny) per week. In 1880, a new law stated that all children under ten years must attend school, but school places were not made free of charge until 1891. Like Stanton Elementary School which 'Maggie' attended in the programmes, many of these schools were called board schools, as they were run by a 'board' of local people. Classes were very large, desks were strictly arranged in rows and severe punishments, such as caning, or 'finger stocks', were given to children who misbehaved. Many schools operated a monitor system, where the younger children were taught by older pupils.

The lessons mainly concentrated on what was called the 'Three Rs' – reading, writing and arithmetic. There were also some lessons in which girls and boys were separated. Girls were taught needlework, while boys practised 'drill', a kind of marching, in the playground. Younger children wrote on slates, using slate pencils. When they finished writing they could rub out their work and use the same slate over again. Older children wrote in ink on paper using a simple pen with a metal nib. They learnt and practised a form of handwriting called 'copperplate'.

Some of the poorer children actually lived in large schools, where they were taught not only to read, but also practical skills like farming or shoemaking. One of the pupils at the Cuckoo Poor School in London was a boy named Charlie Chaplin who grew up to become a very famous film star of the silent movies!

Once each year an inspector came to report on every school in the country. Registers were checked and all pupils were tested. If any children failed the tests, they would have to repeat their last school year all over again with the younger children. If a number of children failed the tests, the teachers would have their pay cut.

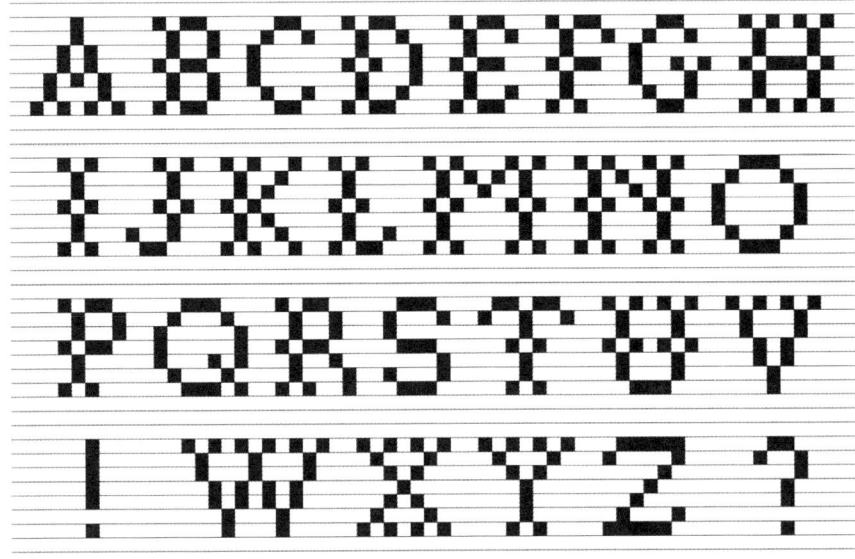

 school log book

A Victorian classroom

Extracts from the log book for Acton Priory School

Feb 7th, 1896	Attendance this week very fair. Standard II – satisfactory results in arithmetic and spelling and all subjects except drill.
Nov 5th, 1897	Attendance rather low owing to a visit by Sander's circus to the town yesterday afternoon, while today a number of boys have gone 'guying'.
Nov 26th, 1897	Attendance lower on account of the bad weather. Yesterday, as the boys were going out to play, a lad named Wilkinson was pushed down the stairs by two other scholars, his leg was hurt so badly that he had to be sent home and is unable to return to school today.

Inspectors' reports for the years 1897 and 1898

The school is well organised, the classwork is satisfactory, with the exception of the grammar of the Fourth Standard. Elementary subjects are well taught, but handwriting does not appear to be over good, especially in the first class.

School visited under Article 84b. The organisation, tone and order are very creditable, the work is well in hand. The teacher of Standard IIa should try to infuse more life into his work.

F. Webb, Sub-Inspector.

opperplate writing

Look at these examples of Victorian children's copperplate handwriting.
Why do you think these sentences were chosen for children to copy and learn?
Can you copy out these sentences in copperplate handwriting?

Too many cooks spoil the broth.

Time and tide wait for no man.

Least said, soonest mended.

Little wealth, little care.

A VICTORIAN DIARY
PROGRAMME 2

Downstairs, Upstairs

Programme outline

Maggie has left school and begins a new life as a junior housemaid at Pockerley Manor – a large house in the north of England. The hours are long, the work is hard, but worse still, Maggie meets up with her old adversary Susan Bailey, who is also employed at the house. After some items of jewellery belonging to the lady of the house go missing, Maggie is falsely accused of theft and dismissed without references.

Learning outcomes

Children should gain an understanding of:

- the servants' way of life in Victorian times
- the differences between the lives of servants and those of their masters
- what a census return is, and what can be learned from it
- the typical features of Victorian houses and styles of decoration

Before viewing

☐ Bring into the classroom some examples of modern domestic appliances such as an iron, an electric kettle and a vacuum cleaner. Pictures of larger items, such as washing machines, may also be useful. Ask the children how washing, cleaning and other chores might have been undertaken 100 years ago. Who would have carried out these tasks in a large Victorian house? Try to get hold of some original Victorian artefacts, such as flat irons or washboards, for comparison. Small items such as irons are often available fairly cheaply from antique stalls or shops. In addition, many museums are able to lend artefacts to schools – see **Additional resources** (page 28).

Whilst viewing

☐ Ask the children to make a list of all the tasks Maggie has to perform during the day, and what equipment she uses to help her.

After viewing

History

☐ Discuss with the children the notes they have made. Ask them to use these notes and the information contained in the **factfile** (page 11) to compile a timetable of Maggie's day, from 5.30 a.m. when she gets up until bedtime. Then ask the children to construct a similar timetable for Mrs Higgins, the head housekeeper, showing how she might have spent her day.

☐ Ask the children to study the census return from 1891 on **Activity sheet 3** (page 12), then discuss this document as a group. Key points could include the number of people listed on the sheet, and how many of these were employed in domestic service. Ask the children to record the information using graphs or, better still, on a computer database. Can they find out what some of the jobs might have entailed? How many people do they imagine might be employed in domestic service in any particular street today? Archive census material is often available in local libraries. Perhaps the children could find the census information for 1871 or 1891 relating to their own area, and, by carrying out a simple survey, compare it with information about life and employment today.

☐ In her *Book of Household Management* published in 1861, Mrs Beeton stated that, 'engaging servants is a most important and onerous duty of the mistress. One of the commonest ways of filling vacancies is to insert an advertisement in a newspaper.' Ask the children to compose an advert for a housemaid's job at Pockerley Manor. Maggie would have been paid the sum of £15 a year.

- Advertisements from the Victorian period can tell us a lot about daily life. Look carefully at **Activity sheet 4** (page 13). What do these adverts claim? Would they be effective? Ask the children to compare these with advertisements for similar products in magazines today. What similarities and differences can they find?

English

- When she invited her guests to dinner, Mrs Willoughby would have used a particularly formal wording on her invitations:

> *Mr & Mrs Willoughby kindly request the pleasure of your company at dinner on the evening of the 18th of November 1880 at 8 o'clock.*
>
> *R.S.V.P.*

Invite the children to use this wording to design their own invitation cards for the Willoughby's dinner party. Encourage them to use copperplate handwriting in their designs.

Art and design

- The Victorian period saw huge growth in the size of many towns and cities. The architecture of houses and public buildings had a distinctive style, with elaborate decorative features often prominently displayed on the outside. Try to arrange a class visit to a local Victorian building. (Perhaps your school is such a building.) The children can sketch the building, showing the external features. What do they think are the most imposing or grand parts of the design? If the building was a house, who do they think lived there in the nineteenth century? (Local census archive material may again be helpful in answering this question.)

- The artist William Morris was one of the first designers to commercially produce patterned wallpaper for large Victorian houses. Some of these patterns are still available in wallpaper shops today, and are also used in wrapping paper designs. The children could study a William Morris design and draw an enlarged section of it using a viewfinder. They can then reproduce their drawings using paint on paper or, if available, using gutta and silk paint on a piece of silk. Alternatively, the design can be etched onto a polystyrene art tile, then dipped in paint or ink to produce a repeated pattern.

- As a follow-up activity, ask the children to each provide a large cardboard box. They can then decorate the inside of the box, using any combination of art materials, reproducing the features of a Victorian room. If the boxes are of a similar size, the finished 'rooms' can be joined together to make a Victorian doll's house.

factfile

Domestic service

Most Victorian households employed servants. A large house like Pockerley Manor would have employed many people, ranging from scullery maids and boot boys, aged 10 or 11, who washed up, peeled potatoes and polished boots, right up to a butler and a housekeeper, who supervised the junior staff.

A housemaid like Maggie would have started work when she was 12 or 13 years old. She would have earned about 7s 6d (37p) a week plus her food, with possibly one afternoon and evening off each week.

Her working day would have begun at 5.30 or 6.00 a.m. She would have started by drawing up the blinds, sweeping the floors, blackleading the grates and laying the fires. She would then have swept the stairs and served breakfast. After breakfast she'd have had to empty the slops, carry water for washing and make the beds. She'd then have dusted and polished furniture in the many rooms, often on her knees. When she wasn't cleaning she would have been expected to sew and mend tablecloths and sheets. When evening came she'd have lit fires in the bedrooms, turned down the beds and laid out the nightclothes, before retiring to bed herself, absolutely exhausted!

Servants could give notice to leave their employers' service, but they were entirely dependent on them for a good reference. Without one, they were unlikely to find another job.

A Victorian hearth

census return

Administrative County of **Middx**		Municipal Borough of			Municipal Ward of		The undermentioned Houses are situated within the Boundaries of the			Urban Sanitary District of **Ealing**		Town or Village or Hamlet of **Ealing**		Sanitary District of		Parliamentary Borough or Division of **Ealing**	Ecclesiastical Parish or District of **St. Mary's**	Page 26

Cols. 1	2	3	4	5	6	7	8	9	10	11	12	13	14	15	16
No. of Schedule	ROAD, STREET, Etc and No. or NAME of HOUSE	HOUSES In-habited (U), or Un-inhabited (U.), or Building (B.)		Number of rooms occu-pied if less than five	NAME and Surname of each Person	RELATION to Head of Family	CONDI-TION as to Marriage	AGE last Birthday Male	AGE last Birthday Female	PROFESSION or OCCUPATION	Employer	Employed	Neither Employer nor Employed	WHERE BORN	If (1) Deaf-and-Dumb (2) Blind (3) Lunatic, Imbecile or Idiot
	Gunnersbury Lane				Alice Makerley	Serv.	S		24	Housemaid (Domestic)				Glos. Cirencester	
164	Manor House				Elizabeth Coll	Serv.	Wid.		31	Cook (Dom.)				Herts. Hitchin	
					T. A. Gleddanes	Head	M.	72		Underwriter				Ireland	
					Elizabeth	Wife	M.		67					Devonshire	
					A. M.	Son	S	39						Middx. London	
					Cyril "	Son	S	38						Middx. London	
					Barbara Laird	Dau.	S		31					Aberdeen	
					Florence Deans	Serv.	S		20	Domestic				Birmingham	
					Corina Shepherd	Serv.	S		50	Domestic				London, Knightsbridge	
					John Ball	Serv.	S	20		Butler, Dom.				Wilts.	
165	Garden Cottage				Richard Mansey	Head	M.	53		Gardener, Dom				London, Paddington	
					Mary Mansey	Wife	M.		59					York, Harrogate	
166	Garden Cottage				Herbert Denison	Head	S	25		Gardener				Oxon, Claydon	
167	Gunnersbury Lodge (Gate)				Rachel Beaumont	Head	Wid.		73	Lodge Keeper				Somersetshire	
					Emily Beaumont	Daughter	S		47					London, Paddington	
					John W. Beaumont	Son	M.	45		Piano-Forte Tuner				London, Paddington	
					Frank H. Beaumont	Son	S	36		Mercantile Clerk				London, Ealing	
					Rosalind Beaumont	Daughter	M.		33					London, Campden	
					Emma Murray	Niece	S		17					Ireland, Dublin	
168	Gunnersbury House				Emily Maria?	Head	Wid.		68					London	
					George Baker	Serv.	S	45		Butler, domestic				London	
					Mary Eacon	Serv.	S		47	Cook, domestic				Somersetshire	
					Alice Mary	Serv.	S		23	Housemaid, domestic				Somersetshire	
					Emily Poole	Serv.	S		23	Housemaid, domestic				Somersetshire	
					Mary Bennet	Serv.	S		22	Kitchenmaid, domestic				Somersetshire	
					John Manning	Serv.	S	20		Footman, domestic				Middx. Acton	
169	Garden Lodge				Chas. Tappin	Head	Wid.	73		Gardener, domestic				Bucks. Amersham	
					Ellen E. Tappin	Dau.	S		29					Middx. Ealing	
Total of Houses and of Tenements with less than Five Rooms					Total of Males and Females			10	18						

Advertisements

CONJURING TRICKS.

PUZZLES.

WONDERFUL AUTOMATA.

HEADS AND FIGURES FOR VENTRILO-QUISM.

ELECTRICAL TRICKS.

BOOK ON CHAPEAUGRAPHY or 25 Heads under one Hat, 1/3, post free.

BOXES OF CONJURING TRICKS, 2/6, 5/6, 10/6, 15/-, 21/-, to 10 guineas.

BOXES OF PUZZLES, 2/6, 5/-, 10/6, 21/-, & 43/-

BOXES OF CARD TRICKS, 2/6, 5/6, 10/6, 21/-, & 42/-

BOX OF SHADOW-GRAPHY, Complete with Apparatus Price 3/9, post free.

ENTERTAINMENTS FOR EVENING PARTIES.

PROFESSOR BLAND'S MAGICAL PALACE OF CONJURING WONDERS,
35, NEW OXFORD STREET, LONDON, W.C.
(Opposite Mudie's Library.)

SUPERIOR LESSONS GIVEN IN LEGERDEMAIN FROM 3 GUINEAS THE COURSE OF 7.

Catalogue of Conjuring Tricks, 6d., post free.   Supplement of Novelties, 1d., post free.

Consumption

can only be cured by using great care in daily life and taking, in addition to ordinary food, such nourishment as will counteract the waste of the disease and give vital strength. For this extra nourishment there is nothing so beneficial as

Scott's Emulsion

If the disease is just developing, Scott's Emulsion will almost always effect a permanent cure. In the last stages of the disease there is more ease and comfort in Scott's Emulsion than any other known remedy. Scott's Emulsion contains curative properties that are effective in all forms of inflammation of Throat and Lungs.

For Coughs, Colds, Sore Throat, Weak Lungs, Bronchitis, Consumption, Emaciation, Loss of Flesh and all

Wasting Diseases of Children.

Always remember when you buy Scott's Emulsion that its formula has been endorsed by physicians for *twenty years*. It is not a secret compound. The only genuine Scott's Emulsion has our trade-mark on *salmon-colored wrapper*.

We shall be pleased to send you our book on "Points." FREE.

SCOTT & BOWNE, (Ltd.), London.   All Chemists, 2/6 and 4/6.

A VICTORIAN DIARY
PROGRAMME 3

Down but not Out

Programme outline

Having lost her position as a maid at Pockerley Manor, Maggie goes to London by train to seek her fortune. She is despondent after several rejections but is then befriended by a Londoner called Bessie. Bessie takes Maggie to work at the Bryant and May match factory in east London, where no references are required. Working conditions are very harsh. On a day off, Maggie and Bessie visit a photographer's shop. Bessie has her portrait taken and Maggie catches the eye of the proprietor Mr Carter.

Susan Bailey, Maggie's old adversary, then reappears as a worker at the factory. Bessie is taken ill with suspected 'phossy jaw' and Maggie is sacked from Bryant and May. She is suspected of passing on information to Annie Besant, a woman who has been fighting the cause of women in appalling working conditions and writing critical accounts of the factory in a newspaper called 'The Link'.

Learning outcomes

Children should gain an understanding of:

- the impact of the railways
- the growth of cities
- working and living conditions in Victorian London

Before viewing

- Recap with the pupils what had happened to Maggie at the end of Programme 2. How do they think she will be able to get a job without a letter of reference or good character? Discuss the impact of the growth of the railway network in the nineteenth century. Before this development many people would have lived all their lives in the same town or village. Brainstorm the advantages and disadvantages of this new form of transport. How could it transform the lives of people like Maggie?

Whilst viewing

- Ask the pupils to make notes of the things that they feel were wrong about the working conditions at Bryant and May in the 1880s.

After viewing

English

- Discuss with the class the notes they made whilst viewing the programme. Compile a list of complaints about the factory. These might include poor wages, unsafe conditions, workers' fines, lack of medical care or compensation for injuries and danger from phosphorus.

English: drama

- Tell the children they are going to participate in a role-play debate. Give each class member a character role. These would include factory workers, concerned members of the public, Annie Besant and her supporters, owners of the factory and foremen. Invite everyone to a meeting to discuss the conditions at Bryant and May, chaired 'in role' by you. Try not to let opinions get too heated or personal!

English: writing

- At the end of the drama session, ask the children to draft a letter to a Member of Parliament using the writing frame on **Activity sheet 5** (page 17), expressing their views on this subject. A neat copy could then be written or word-processed.

History

- One consequence of the development of the railways was a huge shift in the population away from the countryside to the cities. The population in London increased as follows:

  1861 – 3 million
  1881 – 5 million
  1901 – 6 ½ million

  As an ICT activity, ask the children to show this information in the form of a graph.

Then, writing in pairs, list the amenities that would be needed in a Victorian city to cater for this increase in population. This would include housing, water, food, transport and sanitation. Discuss what would happen if these changes did not keep pace with the growth in population. Infectious diseases, such as cholera and consumption (tuberculosis), were all common at the time.

D & T

- With the children read the **factfile** (page 16) about Victorian working and living conditions. Discuss what they know about the features of Victorian living conditions.

  Ask the children to look at the houses on **Activity sheet 6** (page 18). Then ask them in pairs to design and make a model of a Victorian house. They could even make a town or village like that planned by Sir Titus Salt for his workers in Yorkshire.

factfile

Victorian living and working conditions

Many adults and children worked and lived in dreadful conditions in Victorian times. Factory workers worked long hours for small wages, and many workers were injured, sometimes catching hands or arms in the machines.

The Bryant and May match factory

Their homes were usually cramped. Rows of houses were often built 'back to back', each house having one room downstairs and one room upstairs. These rooms were shared by large numbers of people. Some houses did not have their own toilets and to collect water, many families would go to a stand-pipe in the street. Diseases such as typhoid and cholera killed many people in Victorian times, especially children, as drains carrying sewage were emptied straight into the rivers. This was where most people obtained water for washing and drinking.

Some Victorian Christian businessmen such as Sir Titus Salt and George Cadbury were shocked by these living conditions. They decided to build new villages for their workers where everything was clean and healthy. Houses were larger with toilets and running water. There was also access to a church, school and park.

A Victorian hallway

Letter writing

1880

Dear Sir,

I am writing to express my opinion about the working conditions at Bryant and May match factory in east London.

I feel that...

Furthermore,...

Therefore, I think you should...

Yours faithfully,

A VICTORIAN DIARY
PROGRAMME 4

Strike

Programme outline

Maggie begins her new career as a photographer's assistant to Jim Carter. She meets Annie Besant who comes to the studio to ask for her help in writing more articles about Bryant and May. Bessie then brings news from the factory that all the workers have come out on strike! Maggie agrees to become part of the newly formed strike committee. Support is running high, but somehow the management learn about their plans. They discover it is Susan Bailey who has been passing on information and she leaves the committee in disgrace. After one month's struggle, the matchworkers win their dispute and the factory owners agree to all the demands. At the end of the programme there is more happy news when photographer Jim Carter asks Maggie to marry him.

Learning outcomes

Children should gain an understanding of:

- important developments in Victorian employment and social history
- changes in the lives and roles of working women
- the impact of photography

Before viewing

- ☐ Ask the children to make a list of jobs they think were performed by women in Victorian England. Have they included brickmakers, coal miners (in the early part of the period), or photographers' assistants in their list?

Whilst viewing

- ☐ Pause the programme to discuss the advantages of having a female assistant in a photographic studio. This would be important, particularly when photographing Victorian women, who would have their clothing and pose arranged by the assistant. Note that, at the time, even a glimpse of ankle would be seen as shocking!

After viewing

English

- ☐ Read with the class the **factfile** (page 21) describing the events of the matchgirls' strike. Remind them of the structure of a play script and ask them to use their imagination to write a radio play about the strike. Encourage them to work in groups and to use instruments to create sound effects. When complete, record and play them to an audience (perhaps a parallel class in the same age group).

- ☐ Ask the class to use reference materials from books or computer programs to complete notes for a biography of a famous Victorian, using the writing frame on **Activity sheet 7** (page 22). Ask the children to use these drafts to make small, illustrated books. These books might be read by other members of the class, and assessed in terms of their factual content and interest factor.

History

- ☐ As a follow-up activity, try playing 'Who am I?' Write the name of one famous Victorian on the board above a child's head. He or she then has to guess the name of this person by asking ten questions to the rest of the class. They can only reply yes or no!

- ☐ Look at the portrait photographs on **Activity sheet 8** (page 23). They are taken from *The Picture Magazine*, December 1894. Ask the pupils what they tell us about Victorian women. Importantly, what do they <u>not</u> tell us about the lives of many women during this period?

Ask the class to invent thought or speech bubbles for the women in the photographs. They may be humorous or serious! Try arranging a typical backdrop for a Victorian studio portrait. Include a table or chair with a plant, a book or teapot. The children could dress up in Victorian costume and have their photographs taken with suitably solemn expressions, using a black and white or sepia film. To form a striking contrast, try mounting them with colour photographs of the children in their usual clothes.

Photography

☐ The invention of photography allowed people in Victorian Britain to see other people, animals and places that they had not seen before.

Photography became a popular new art form in the Victorian era. Try experimenting with the developing process by creating photograms with the class. (These are photographic images produced without using a camera.) To achieve this you will need:

- A darkened area (a walk-in cupboard with any windows blacked out works well)
- A light source (a photographic enlarger or a lamp with a 100-watt bulb and a black reflector or shade)
- 4 x plastic trays
- Photographic paper ⎫
- Developing fluid and fixer ⎬ both available from photographic shops
- Water
- A piece of glass
- Tongs
- Protective gloves

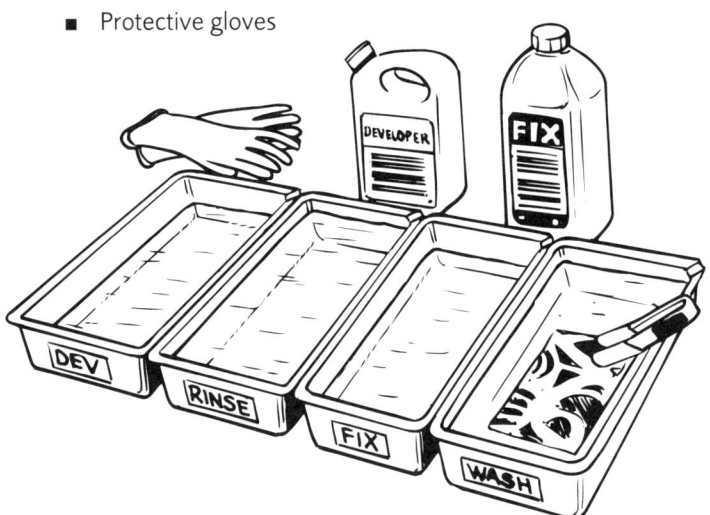

This activity should take place with small numbers of children and be carefully supervised by a responsible adult. The chemicals, used properly, are harmless but should not be allowed to touch the mouth or eyes. Always use the tongs and wash hands after any contact.

1. Place the photographic paper under a piece of glass.
2. Arrange one or more objects on top of the glass.
3. Switch on the light source to expose the paper for 10 seconds. (This time may need to be altered; try a little experimentation.)
4. Wearing gloves and using the tongs, place the exposed paper into a tray of developer fluid and leave for approximately 1½ – 2 mins.
5. When you see the image appear, lift it out with the tongs and place it into a tray of water to rinse off the developer.
6. Lift out with the tongs and place in the tray of fixer for the length of time given on the packet.
7. Lift out again with the tongs and wash all the chemicals away in the final tray or under running water.
8. Leave the finished photograph to dry.

Children become very excited when they see their finished results and can enjoy experimenting using different objects or cutting out shapes from cards. The following example of a photogram is made by children aged 10.

factfile

Factory working conditions

The Deputation.

Three sturdy respectable women soon appeared in the LINK office, and told their story, which, briefly was as follows. The foremen had brought round on Wednesday a paper certifying that the girls were well treated and contented and repudiated the statements made on their condition, and this paper was laid to receive signatures during the dinner hour. When the foreman of one department returned, expecting to find it filled, it offered to his angry eyes a white unsullied surface. In vain he threatened and scolded; the girls would not sign; as one of them said to Annie Besant in recounting the story, "You had spoke up for us and we weren't going back on you". A girl pitched on apparently as ringleader was threatened with dismissal, but stood firm. On the following morning she was suddenly discharged for a pretended act of insubordination, and the women, promptly seeing the reason of her punishment, put down their work with one accord and marched out. The news spread, and the rest of the wood-match girls followed their example, some 1,400 women suddenly united in a common cause. An offer was made to take back the girl, but the spirit of revolt against cruel oppression had been aroused, and they declared they would not go in "without their pennies".

In July 1888, 1,400 'matchgirls' who worked at Bryant and May's match factory in east London caused a sensation when they went out on strike. A woman called Annie Besant had written about the awful conditions at the factory in a newspaper called *The Link*.

During the strike, she helped to organize support and strike pay for the workers and had questions asked in Parliament about their working conditions.

After one month on strike, the employers gave in to their demands. These were:

- Higher wages
- Shorter hours
- A room to eat food away from the phosphorus
- A dental surgery
- No deductions to their pay
- Setting up of a union

The Union of Women Matchmakers was born and the women had won a great victory for workers' rights.

 Victorian biography

A biography of ....

He/she was born in ....(year)

At .... (place)

He/she is famous because he/she ....

....

An important thing that happened to him/her was ....

....

This occurred in .... at ....

He/she died in ....

I think he/she was important because ....

....

Alexander Bell

Queen Victoria

Florence Nightingale

The Picture Magazine

Miss Maude Millet

Mrs Bernard Beere

Mrs Bancroft

Miss Marion Terry

A VICTORIAN DIARY
PROGRAMME 5

Final Chapter

Programme outline

In the final episode we see Maggie's fortunes flourishing. She is married to Jim, has two children, Maud and Alice, and the photography business is booming. She and her family witness some of the innovations and events of the late nineteenth century – they acquire a telephone, watch some of the new 'moving pictures' and take part in Queen Victoria's Diamond Jubilee celebrations.

As fate would have it, Maggie meets up with Susan Bailey once more. Susan's life has taken a very different turn – she is now destitute and has taken to begging on the streets. As Maggie tries to offer Susan some help, Alice chases her ball into the path of an oncoming horse-drawn tram! Susan reacts quickly and manages to push Alice to safety, but, in doing so, is herself knocked down by the tram. A doctor sees Susan immediately but he can do nothing to save her life and, sadly, she dies. She is buried with the epitaph: 'She paid her debts'.

The series ends as it began, with Maggie writing her diary at the dawn of the new century.

Learning outcomes

Children should gain an understanding of:

- the importance of the Victorian era in advancing new technology and invention
- the chronological sequence of events during the Victorian age
- Victorian forms of entertainment
- the structure of a story

Before viewing

- ☐ Discuss with the children the elements of story structure. A story usually includes a beginning (describing a person or a place), a middle (where a problem or conflict arises) and an ending. Endings sometimes resolve the problem, or may take the form of an anticlimax, and sometimes can include a 'twist' in the tale. Can the class predict how Maggie's story will end?

Whilst viewing

- ☐ The Victorian period was 'great' in terms of the advancement of design and technology. Ask the children to note down any inventions they spot during the course of the programme.

After viewing

English

- ☐ Discuss, with the children, the lists of new inventions they have made, and also Maggie's reactions to the new forms of technology. What modern inventions do they think Maggie would be astonished by if she were alive today? What would she have said had she been told that, within seventy years, a man would walk on the moon?

- ☐ Ask the children to plot some nineteenth-century inventions on the timeline on **Activity sheet 9** (page 27). Suggest that the children carry out some further research on some of these inventions and their inventors, so that they can answer these key questions:

- Who was the inventor?
- What country did he/she come from?
- Was it a success straightaway?
- Why were there so few women inventors?

Ask the children to present their findings in the form of a 'zig zag' book, or as an illustrated page of information which might be used in a computer program, or on a CD-ROM.

☐ To complete this topic, ask the children to work in pairs to design an illustrated poster showing an invention to improve the life of someone living a hundred years from now. Ask them to explain what their invention will be made of, and what it will do!

English: writing

☐ Suggest that the children summarize what they have learnt about the Victorians.

☐ In the programme, the words: 'She paid her debts' on Susan's epitaph, take a moral tone. As an extended writing activity ask the children to write a 'morality' tale which delivers a message to the reader about an issue which is important today. You may like to read the children excerpts from some well-known Victorian examples, such as *Black Beauty* by Anna Sewell.

History: lifestyle

☐ In Programme 5 we see Maggie and her family enjoying leisure time. Read with the class the **factfile** (page 26) about Victorian entertainment and pastimes. Ask the children to use one colour to highlight pastimes that are still enjoyed today, and a different colour for pastimes confined to the Victorian era. What do the children conclude?

History: past and present

☐ Finally, Jim's photographs attempted to show aspects of Victorian life. Take the class for a walk in your local area with a camera. Encourage the children to capture some images of life at the end of the twentieth century. What do they think people will make of these photographs a hundred years from now? How much of what they see might remain the same?

D & T

☐ Stories read and games played by Victorian children often had moral messages or lessons built into them. The board game shown in the programme has a square bearing the message: 'Late!... go back to 44' and another saying 'Promptness! – advance to being a clerk'. Ask the children in groups to design and make a board game introducing some of the advantages and disadvantages of Victorian life. One square might say 'Cholera epidemic – go back five spaces', whilst another might announce 'Electricity arrives! – go forward four spaces'.

factfile

Victorian entertainment and leisure

In an age without television and video, Victorian families made their own entertainment. Children from less wealthy families often played in the streets with hoops, skipping ropes, marbles, buttons or footballs. Dolls were popular and could be cheaply made from everyday objects such as clothes pegs, or even old boots! Children in wealthy households often had many expensive toys, including board games, rocking horses, mechanical toys and model soldiers.

Optical toys such as zoetropes and 'magic' lanterns also became popular as people began to be fascinated by optical illusions. Zoetropes, when spun, made still pictures appear to move, while 'magic' lanterns worked in a similar way to modern slide projectors, often showing scenes from well-known children's stories.

Wealthy adults entertained themselves by singing, playing the piano and by reading aloud to each other. Theatres and music halls were popular places to visit – there you might watch anything from serious dramas and musical recitals, to conjuring tricks and comedy singing acts.

In 1871 the Bank Holiday Act gave all workers a number of guaranteed holidays each year. As the railway network grew, people began to spend their holidays travelling to seaside resorts like Blackpool, where they would bathe in the sea. Ladies would be wheeled into the sea in special bathing machines that looked like wooden carriages, so that they would not be seen in their swimming costumes!

A zoetrope

Inventions of the century

1885 – Safety bicycle manufactured

1839 – First photographic prints

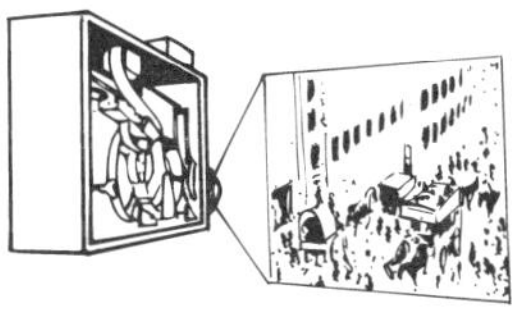

1879 – First electric light bulb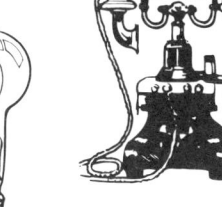

1896 – Moving pictures first seen in Britain

1876 – Telephone invented

1840 – Postage stamps invented

1850 – Early washtub

1879 – First flushing public toilet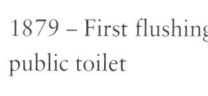

1879 – First toothpaste in tubes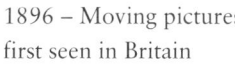

Mark the inventions on the timeline below.

1830

1837 – *Victoria becomes Queen*

1840

1850

1860

1870

1880

1890

1900

1910

A VICTORIAN DIARY

Additional resources

Places to visit

Beamish Open Air Museum, Beamish, Co. Durham DH9 0RG (tel. 01207 231811)

The Ragged School Museum, Copperfield Road, London E3 4RR (tel. 020 7232 2941)

Gunnersbury Park Museum, Gunnersbury Park, London W3 8LQ (tel. 020 8992 1612)

Abbeydale Industrial Museum, Abbeydale Road South, Sheffield (tel. 0114 236 7731)

The Museum of Childhood, 42 High Street, Royal Mile, Edinburgh (tel. 0131 529 4142)

The Black Country Museum, Tipton Road, Dudley, West Midlands (tel. 0121 557 9643)

Blists Hill Victorian Town Museum, Ironbridge Gorge Museum, Ironbridge, Telford, Shropshire (tel. 01952 433522)

Background reading for teachers

Solidarity – Women History Makers by A. Sproule (pub. MacDonald & Co. 1987)

Faith in History by M. Cooling (pub. Eagle 1988)

Mrs Beeton's Book of Household Management (first pub. 1861)

Victorian Britain, 1837 – 1901, KS2 Core Study (P.J. Publications 1994)

The Rise and Fall of the Victorian Servant by P. Horn (pub. Sutton Publishing)

Matchgirls' Strike, 1888 by R. Beer (available from National Museum of Labour History, Limehouse Town Hall, Commercial Road, London E14)

Resource packs and books for pupils

Pupil resources, loan boxes & archive reproduction packs available from Beamish Museum

'Entertaining the Victorians' – pack available from Education Dept., Museum of the Moving Image, South Bank, Waterloo, London SE1 8XT

'Victorian Childhood Factpack' – edited by C. Makepeace, Elm Publications, 12 Blackstone Road, Huntingdon, Cambridgeshire (tel. 01480 414 553)

Publications on the Victorian household and Victorian childhood available from Gunnersbury Park Museum, Gunnersbury Park, London W3 8LQ (tel. 020 8992 2247)

The Diary of Anne Frank (pub. Pan Books)

The Angel of Nitshill Road by Anne Fine (pub. Egmont Childrens Books)

The Wreck of the Zanzibar by Michael Morpurgo (pub. Mammoth)